Ex Libris

J.E. JENNINGS

2014

PROFILES OF FLIGHT

PANAVIA TORNADO

F.2 ZA254, the first of three air-defence variant (ADV) prototypes, with six semi-recessed Sky Flash missiles under the lengthened fuselage, with Foxhunter radar in the nose. Developed from the Tornado IDS for a wholly RAF requirement, the ADV was optimised for long-range interception. The F.2 was an interim aircraft which initially equipped the OCU, but never entered squadron service. (BAe)

PROFILES OF FLIGHT

PANAVIA TORNADO

STRIKE, ANTI-SHIP, AIR SUPERIORITY, AIR DEFENCE, RECONNAISSANCE
AND ELECTRONIC WARFARE FIGHTER-BOMBER

DAVE WINDLE & MARTIN BOWMAN

Pen & Sword
AVIATION

First published in Great Britain in 2010 by
PEN & SWORD AVIATION
An imprint of
Pen & Sword Books Ltd
47 Church Street
Barnsley
South Yorkshire
S70 2AS

Copyright © Dave Windle & Martin W. Bowman, 2010

ISBN 978 1 84884 235 9

The right of Dave Windle & Martin W. Bowman to be identified as Authors of this
work has been asserted by them in accordance with the Copyright, Designs and
Patents Act 1988.

A CIP catalogue record for this book is
available from the British Library

Printed in China through Printworks Int. Ltd

Pen & Sword Books Ltd incorporates the Imprints of
Pen & Sword Aviation, Pen & Sword Family History, Pen & Sword Maritime,
Pen & Sword Military, Wharncliffe Local History, Pen & Sword Select,
Pen & Sword Military Classics, Leo Cooper, Remember When,
Seaforth Publishing and Frontline Publishing

For a complete list of Pen & Sword titles please contact
PEN & SWORD BOOKS LIMITED
47 Church Street, Barnsley, South Yorkshire, S70 2AS, England
E-mail: enquiries@pen-and-sword.co.uk
Website: www.pen-and-sword.co.uk

ACKNOWLEDGEMENTS

I am indebted to Bernard Noble and his son Kevin Noble for their kind permission to adapt material from *Noble Endeavours (Three Generations of RAF Pilots)* (1998), which details the varied and successful careers of both these remarkable RAF pilots. The vivid descriptions of Tornado operations and training have been adapted from this family 'bible'. Bernard joined the RAF as an apprentice in 1946, and was a serving RAF officer until retirement in 1994 with the rank of squadron leader. Prior to joining the Tornado force, Kevin Noble was a Jaguar pilot in RAF Germany, and this period of his remarkable career is featured in *SEPECAT Jaguar: Tactical Support & Maritime Strike Fighter* by Martin W. Bowman (Pen & Sword 2007). His earlier career on the BAe Hawk is also featured in the *Profiles of Flight* series. At the time of writing Kevin is a 747 commercial airline captain with British Airways. I am also most grateful to BAe; Ed Bulpett; MBB; Nigel McTeer, Tony Paxton and Graham Simons of GMS.

A Tornado being prepared for flight at RAF Cottesmore. Behind is 43+01 'G-21'. (GMS)

PANAVIA TORNADO

In 1965 British Aircraft Corporation (BAC) and Dassault agreed to collaborate on an AFVG (Anglo-French Variable Geometry) proposal, and a Memorandum of Understanding was signed on 17 May 1965. The AFVG was to be a multi-role aircraft for use by the air forces and naval air arms of both Britain and France. A full-scale mock-up was assembled at BAC Warton, but on 29 June 1967 France withdrew from the project and the UK government sought out other likely European partners for a collaborative aircraft project designated MRA-75 (Multi-Role Aircraft for 1975). Germany and Italy joined the Tornado programme after a meeting on 19 October 1967 at Fürstenfeldbruck, near Munich, when the Chiefs of Staff of the Belgian, Dutch, West German and Italian air forces met to discuss a possible replacement for their Lockheed F-104 Starfighters. In Britain the main purpose of the Interdictor Strike (IDS) version was to provide a replacement for the Vulcan and Buccaneer and Canberra in the overland strike, maritime strike and reconnaissance roles respectively. An air-defence variant would replace the Phantoms and Lightnings in both the UK and Germany.

In July 1970 the British and West German governments went

P.04 D-9542, the fourth Tornado prototype, which first flew on 2 September 1975, firing a Kormoran anti-ship missile. P.01, the first prototype (D-9591) flew on 14 August 1974. D-9542 was destroyed in a flying accident in April 1980, killing both crew. (MBB)

7

ahead with a Multi-Role Combat Aircraft (MRCA), and they were joined two months later by Italy. On 26 March 1969 a new multi-national company, Panavia GmbH, had been formed in Munich to oversee the activities of Aeritalia of Turin in Italy, BAC at Warton and Messerschmitt-Bölkow-Blohm (MBB) at Augsburg in West Germany, who would jointly build the new aircraft. BAC and MBB each took a 42.5% share in the new company. In Italy Fiat took a 15% share (in June the Netherlands pulled out of the programme).

P.02 XX946, the second Tornado prototype, which first flew on 30 October 1974, with a Handley Page Victor K2 tanker during early trials. (BAe)

P.13 (98+02), the fifth German aircraft, and one of the six pre-series Tornado aircraft (P.11-P.16), which first flew on 10 January 1978. (MBB)

In September 1969 Turbo-Union, a consortium of Rolls-Royce (40%), MTU (40%) and Fiat (20%), was formed to build and develop the Rolls-Royce RB-199-34R three-spool turbofan to power the MRCA. Aircraft in the initial production batches were powered by the Mk 101 variant, which developed 9,000 lb of thrust in 'cold' power and was boosted to 16,000 lb of thrust with reheat, which meant that the aircraft was underpowered in dry thrust, especially at altitude, and it required the use of afterburner to give it reasonable performance. Later Tornadoes were fitted with the more powerful Mk 103 version of the RB-199-34R engine. Front and rear fuselage manufacture was the responsibility of BAC (later British Aerospace) at Warton, the wings being built by Aeritalia, while responsibility for the manufacture of the centre fuselage section was undertaken by MBB (later Deutsche Aerospace SA). Final assembly of the aircraft was undertaken at the national aircraft manufacturing plants relevant to the air forces for which the aircraft were destined.

Britain, Germany and Italy signed a Memorandum of Understanding on MRCA in 1970, and placed contracts for ten prototype MRCA aircraft. In April 1973 the construction of six pre-series aircraft was agreed. The first aircraft (MRCA 01) was assembled in Germany and flew for the first time on 14 August 1974 at Manching. The first flight of the second prototype took place from Warton on 30 October 1974. By the end of March 1976 the seventh prototype was flying. That same month the Panavia 200 Multi-Role Combat Aircraft was named 'Tornado'. On 29 July Britain, Germany and Italy agreed to purchase 809 Tornadoes (385 for the RAF, including 165 of the ADV air-defence version; 202 for the *Luftwaffe*, replacing the F-104G and G.91R; 122 for the *Marineflieger*, replacing the F-104G; and 100 for the *Regia Aeronautica*, replacing the F-104G and G.91Y) in all roles. The first public flight of the Tornado was at the SBAC show at Farnborough in September 1976, where Tornado 06 was demonstrated. The first delivery of Tornadoes was to begin in 1979 to the Tri-National Operational Conversion Unit at RAF Cottesmore. The first production aircraft for use by the 'Triple T-E' was delivered on 1 July 1980. Initial deliveries to the air arms of West Germany, Italy and the UK were made in the period 1982/3. The first German unit to receive the Tornado was the joint Air Force & Navy Weapons Conversion Unit in 1982. Later that same year the first operational Tornadoes for the German Navy were based with *Marineflieger Geschwader 1* at Jagel. The first Tornadoes operational with the *Luftwaffe* were assigned to *Jagdbombergeschwader 31* late in 1983. In August 1982 the first Tornadoes entered service with the Italian Air Force when *154° Gruppo* received eighteen aircraft. By 1986 German contracts for the Tornado stood at 324, of which 228 were assigned to the *Luftwaffe*. After the original production requirements were formalised, new orders included nine more Tornadoes for the RAF, thirty-five of an ECR (Electronic Combat and Reconnaissance) version beginning in 1991 to replace the RF-4E in the *Luftwaffe*, seventy-two for the Royal Saudi Air Force and eight for the Sultan of Oman's air force.

In Britain the Tornado GR1 strike wing became reality on 1 May 1983 when 27 Squadron, the third and final UK-based Tornado interdictor-strike squadron, arrived at Marham. Officially, the date of the squadron's formation was 12 August, by which time a full complement of thirteen Tornadoes had been delivered. In September three 617 Squadron Tornadoes visited Canada, flying

the 3,500-mile journey to the Toronto International Airport with the aid of Victor and Vulcan tankers. On 28 October Tornado ZA558/F of 617 Squadron was lost when it crashed into the sea ten miles north-west of Cromer, Norfolk. The navigator ejected and was uninjured, but the pilot was killed. Between 28 January and 8 February 1984 four of 27 Squadron's Tornadoes were flown to Thumrait airfield in the Gulf Sultanate of Oman for a goodwill visit. The 'Flying Elephants' participated in and won a bombing competition with the Sultan of Oman's Air Force Hunters and Jaguars, and the Tornadoes also visited Abu Dhabi and Saudi Arabia. During a 27 Squadron deployment to Goose Bay in July for Exercise *Western Vortex*, Tornado GR1 ZA494 crashed after a flap problem. The crew ejected safely. In November the squadron lost a second Tornado when the crew ejected safely from ZA603 during a training sortie in Germany. On 8 November 1984 Tornado ZA604 of 27 Squadron was involved in a

Tornado prototype aircraft carrying two underwing 330-gallon drop-tanks and two Sky Shadow dummies. (BAe)

collision with a USAFE A-10A close support aircraft. The crew ejected without injury. The A-10A was landed safely.

In October 1984 617 Squadron took part in the annual US Strategic Air Command Bombing Competition at Ellsworth Air Force Base, South Dakota. The Dam Busters' six Tornadoes needed tanker support provided by 55 Squadron's Victors to compete in Exercise *Prairie Vortex* against B-52s of Strategic Air Command and F-111s of the Tactical Air Command. F-111Cs of the Royal Australian Air Force also took part. In total forty-two crews were

competing for three trophies. The competition involved two phases of bombing sorties over the low-level ranges in Montana, Nevada, South Dakota and Wyoming, and extended over eight weeks. The first six weeks of the detachment were spent as a work-up period to allow everyone to acclimatise, settle in and sort out the aircraft before the competition proper began. The first phase comprised a single 5¼-hour daylight hi-lo-hi bombing mission, in which terrain following and electronic countermeasures (ECM) were employed to avoid detection and attacks by interceptors and simulated SAMs;

Tornadoes of the Tri-National Tornado Training Establishment (TTTE) at RAF Cottesmore. (GMS)

live practice bombs were dropped on invisible targets using offset blind-bombing techniques. A low-level dash and high-level cruise return completed the mission. Phase 2 involved a six-hour mission and was flown over two separate courses, one in daylight and the other at night. Multiple targets were attacked at high and low level using tone bombs while evading multiple threats from interceptors and missiles. Throughout the missions timing was recorded to within one-second accuracy, as was navigation and bombing. It must be remembered that the Tornado was the only aircraft in the competition that demanded in-flight refuelling, by Victor K2 tankers of 55 Squadron, requiring split-second timing to avoid acquiring penalty points. The Tornadoes required at least two AAR brackets per sortie, and in total 111 day and night join-ups were successfully made. The LeMay and Meyer trophies had never been out of the USA before, but 617 Squadron won both of these trophies, and the Mathis was missed only because the radar failed in one of the Tornadoes at a crucial point in the competition. The Curtis E. LeMay Trophy, awarded to the crew with the highest number of points scored in high- and low-level bombing and time control, was won when two 617 Squadron crews gained first and second places. The John C. Meyer Trophy awarded for 'the best low-level damage expectancy' was won by Squadron Leader Dunlop and Flight Lieutenant Middleton with 90.4%, beating an F-111F of the 48th Tactical Fighter Wing by almost four percentage points. Another Tornado was placed third. In the Mathis Trophy awarded to the team with the highest points for both high- and low-level bombing, Tornado crews were placed second and sixth. In thirty timed bomb releases 617 Squadron achieved an average timing error of less than one second. In bombing accuracy during the

high-speed, low-level attacks of both phases, the average mean point of impact was less than twenty yards from the target: during the high-level bombing of Phase 2 the average mean point of impact was twenty-one yards from the target. Richard DeLauer, Under-Secretary of Defence for Research and Engineering in the DoD, had said that the Tornado was 'vulnerable, heavy and expensive. I just don't think it's a good plane'!

In October 1985 six Tornadoes of 27 Squadron, together with Victor tankers of 57 Squadron, competed in that year's Bombing Competition at Ellsworth. The early sorties were designed to be mini-replicas of the competition missions, with both Victors and Tornadoes flying for about 2½ hours in preparation for the 6½-hour competition routes. The whole RAF detachment was supporting two teams in the competition, with two Tornado crews and two Victor crews in each team. Each crew flew three competition sorties spread over three weeks, with no allowance given for mistakes or if aircraft failed to take off on time. The first two Tornado missions were 6½ hours long and covered 2,800 miles over four states of the Mid-West. On each sortie the crew dropped one bomb from medium level and four from low level, while using the Sky Shadow ECM pod to confuse simulated surface-to-air missiles (SAMs). The bombs were electronic 'tone' bombs, where the aircraft generates a tone for weapon release while the aircraft is being tracked by ground-based radar. The radar then calculates where the bomb would have fallen. For the final competition mission the Tornadoes flew a low-level route through the deserts of Utah, Arizona and Nevada to avoid USAF fighters and SAMs before dropping two practice bombs on targets very close together. A complication for the crews was that all the targets were merely map references on

Strapping-in. (GMS)

the ground and had to be attacked using offset aiming techniques. Offset bombing allows the crew to mark a known point either visually or on radar while the aircraft's main computer makes the necessary calculations for the aircraft to bomb the target. Before flight, therefore, the range and bearing of the offset point from the target needed to be accurately calculated in order to give the best bomb scores. Tornado crews took second place in all three trophies and first place in the Meyer and LeMay trophies. In the Meyer Trophy the winning 'team' gained a damage expectancy of 94.97%. Two other crews came second. Tornadoes took first and second places in the Curtis E. LeMay Trophy. Right up to the closing stages 27 Squadron was heading for a clean sweep, and it only needed a moderate score by one aircraft for the Tornadoes to take the first two places in the Mathis Trophy. Unfortunately, over the last target an aircraft had one of its practice bombs 'hang up', and by the rules of the competition its crew was awarded the score of the lowest-

Italian Air Force IDS Tornado MM55001 'I-40' of the Standards Squadron, TTTE, which suffered an undercarriage collapse at RAF Cottesmore during a roller landing on 9 October 1984. (GMS)

placed aircraft, dropping 27 Squadron to second place in the contest.

By 1986 the first interim Tornado F.2 Air Defence Variant aircraft, which initially equipped the OCU, but never entered squadron service, had been replaced by the first of 152 production Tornado F.3s, which were to equip seven UK-based squadrons. Developed from the Tornado IDS for a wholly RAF requirement, the Tornado ADV was optimised for long-range interception. Key features comprised installation of Foxhunter radar and a lengthened fuselage for carriage of semi-recessed Sky Flash medium-range AAMs developed from the American AIM-7 Sparrow missile. The IDS aircraft employs integrated all-weather navigation and weapon-delivery avionics, and a fly-by-wire control system. Central to the Integrated Avionic System is the main computer, which

Tornado 'G-75' after going off the runway during TTTE training at RAF Cottesmore on 5 January 1989. (GMS)

Tornado ZA548 'B-10' of the TTTE, which left the runway at RAF Cottesmore on 28 January 1985. This aircraft first flew on 3 July 1981. (GMS)

handles the following sub-systems and their associated sensors: flight direction and terrain following; navigation; weapon aiming and delivery; computing; communication; defensive measures. The sub-systems are further linked to various sensors and systems, some of which possess their own computing capability; thus, if the main computer goes off-line for any reason, the aircraft is still capable of completing a mission, albeit with downgraded systems. Mounted in the nose radome are the two radar sets, the ground mapping radar (GMR) and the terrain-following radar (TFR). The GMR is the main sensor for blind navigation and attack, and is optimised for low-level, air-to-ground operation to provide high-resolution ground mapping for target and *en route* fixing, as well as to provide the main computer with accurate ranging information for weapon delivery. The TFR provides information for one of the most important features of the Tornado's low-level, high-speed concept of operation, i.e. its all-weather terrain-following capability. The automatic terrain-following system controls the aircraft's flight path to a pre-set height above the ground, and this can be pre-set to between 200 and 1,500 feet. The pilot is able to select from three types of ride while using the auto terrain-following facility – soft, medium and hard. The soft ride 'smoothes' out the ground contours, by not forcing the aircraft into abrupt manoeuvres, while at the extreme setting, the hard ride, the aircraft is commanded to hug the ground terrain, following the contours as closely as possible to exploit their cover.

By August 1988 the Tri-National Tornado Training Establishment (TTTE) at Cottesmore had reached Course 117. One of the eighteen pilots who attended the course was Flight Lieutenant Kevin Noble, who had flown Jaguars in RAF Germany.

The first month was spent in the ground school and flight simulator, as the Tornado GR1 was a very complex machine with a multiplicity of systems. The GR1 had a similar operational role to the Jaguar, but it had all-weather, day-and-night capability and a longer range. A two-seat aircraft, it had approximately twice the weight and thrust of the Jaguar, weighing about 14 tons empty and 30 tons (approaching that of a loaded Lancaster) at maximum load, and, being relatively small, it was densely packed with equipment and fuel. The RB 199 was a relatively small, but complex, three-spool engine, which was very efficient in dry power, using only slightly more fuel than the Jaguar in cruising flight. However, as the Tornado carried much more fuel – about five tons (1,250 gallons) in the internal tanks,

Italian Air Force IDS Tornado MM55001 'I-40' of the Standards Squadron being craned off the runway at RAF Cottesmore. (GMS)

Fire crews spraying foam on a crashed Tornado of TTTE at RAF Cottesmore. (GMS)

with two more (500 gallons) in the normal underwing tanks – the range was much greater. Unfortunately, in A/B consumption was prodigious, with just under half a ton (about 100 gallons) in the fin tank being used during the take-off roll. The 'hot-shot' method of lighting the A/B was employed, extra fuel being squirted into the combustion chamber, sending a tongue of flame back through the three turbines to the afterburner vapour gutters in the jet pipe. This method was not completely reliable, and with its short jet pipe and huge burner it was an extremely noisy engine.

Throttle control was by electrical signalling, there being no mechanical connection between the throttle levers and the engines, and this produced problems. For instance, if total electrical generating failure occurred it was necessary to land

Tornado ZA320 'B-01', which first flew on 14 December 1979, in the engine detuner at RAF Cottesmore. (GMS)

without delay as, once the battery was flat, the engines ran away to destruction – a considerable problem if in mid-Atlantic at the time. Cases even occurred of engines being inadvertently blown up by pilots switching off all electrical power on shut-down before stop-cocking the engines. Unusually for a fighter, the Tornado was fitted with thrust reversers, the Swedish Viggen being about the only other type so equipped. A pair of clamshell buckets above and below the jet pipe on each engine were operated by air motors to deflect the jet flow forwards. After touchdown the throttles were closed to idle to get the nosewheel firmly on the runway before selecting reverse by rocking the throttles outboard and pushing them forward to increase reverse thrust. As the reverse flow impinged on the fin, the use of thrust reversing was destabilising directionally. A nosewheel steering augmentation system was therefore fitted to enable the pilot to keep the aircraft straight and prevent any pilot-induced oscillation on the nosewheel steering, which could cause the aircraft to go off the runway. Basically, thrust reversing was a very good system, but it increased weight and complexity, was sensitive to crosswinds and had many limitations when landing or aborting take-off on one engine because of the large asymmetric effect. However, it was very useful when landing away from base as it removed the requirement for the pilot to repack a braking parachute.

The throttles themselves seemed unnecessarily large and took up much valuable space. Engine temperature was measured by turbine blade temperature (TBT) instead of the more usual jet pipe temperature (JPT). Many of the German and Italian pilots had previously flown the F-4 and F-104, where A/B was selected by rocking the throttles outboard, and inevitably a few did this in error before starting the take-off roll. The result was embarrassing as on the Tornado this deployed the thrust reverser, and if the brakes were still on the aircraft promptly sat on its tail. A good feature of the Tornado was that the hydraulic pumps and electrical generators were powered from inter-connected gearboxes which were driven by both engines or the auxiliary power unit (APU), so that if an engine failed in flight, all services were still available. The primary flying control system was 'fly by wire', which meant that, for normal operation, there was no mechanical interconnection between the cockpit and the powered control surfaces. Instead, a command stability augmentation system (CSAS) caused the pilot's movements of the stick and rudder pedals to send electronic inputs to the flying control computers, which were programmed to take the flight conditions into account, before producing the necessary deflections of the control surfaces. This system provided good aircraft stability and control throughout the speed range, as well as appropriate control feel, and did not become over-sensitive at high speed. Auto-throttle was also provided, which enabled the aircraft to accelerate to and maintain a selected speed (usually 420 knots), as it flew up hill and down dale under TFR control, although most pilots did not use this facility when flying by day.

Position of the variable-sweep (swing) wing was controlled by a large lever next to the throttles, and there were three main settings marked by detents for ease of location. These were 25° for take-off landing and manoeuvre at relatively slow speeds, 45° for cruise and the maximum of 45° for transonic and supersonic flight. After take-off at 25°, sweep was increased to 45° as the aircraft accelerated and normally left at this setting until just before landing. Maximum sweep was not much used on the Tornado GR1, as at low level with external stores the Mach number was rarely high enough to necessitate it, whereas with the F3 operating in the air-defence role it was frequently necessary. Surprisingly, there was little longitudinal trim change as wing sweep was increased or decreased. Each wing swivelled on a single titanium pin, and when pylons were fitted, they all pivoted with the wings to keep the tanks or stores aligned with the airflow. As the wings swept back, the inner trailing edges entered slots in the fuselage which were normally sealed by air bags, using air from the engine compressors, and the flaps had to be retracted before the wings could be swept back into the slots.

Two radars were accommodated in the nose cone. The ground-mapping radar had a large scanner which swept from side to side and mapped features up to eighty miles ahead, provided the aircraft was at high enough altitude. The associated display in the rear cockpit was used by the navigator to locate targets and features for navigational fixes. The much smaller terrain following radar (TFR) was mounted below the main radar, and its scanner nodded up and down, surveying the terrain up to a few miles ahead, its display being mounted in the front cockpit for use by the pilot. The RAF GR1 had a laser ranger and marked target seeker in a fairing under the nose, but German and Italian aircraft did not. The radar homing and warning receiver (RHWR) had a small circular display, showing detected radars by a strobe indicating an accurate bearing. The central warning panel (CWP) was at the bottom of the right instrument panel, below the fuel and engine instruments.

Although the acceleration of the Tornado was not outstanding at the lower speeds, once it was above 450 knots it really seemed to 'take off'. While going through the speed of sound (Mach 1) was pleasantly uneventful, the control and stability augmentation system smoothed out the flying characteristics, and once past Mach 1 the rate of acceleration continued to be very impressive. The price to pay for using the afterburner at high speed and low level was disproportionately high fuel consumption, something of the order of 250 gallons per minute, which was quicker than using the fuel dump system.

Kevin Noble completed the course, and in November 1988 attended the Tornado Weapons Conversion Unit (TWCU) at RAF Honington, Suffolk.

The training weapons were the 3 kg bomb to simulate retarded bombs and the JP233 runway-denial weapon and the 14 kg bomb to simulate normal (slick) bombs. All weapons were carried on pylons. Two long 'shoulder' pylons extended most of the length of the left and right sides of the lower fuselage, and each could carry two bombs in tandem,

Tornadoes in formation from RAF Cottesmore in 1981. The leading aircraft is ZA325 'B-03', which first flew on 8 September 1980, followed by ZA324 'B-02', nearest the camera, which first flew on 25 June 1980, and 43+06 'G-25'. (GMS)

giving a total of four, this being the standard load. Fitting twin-store carriers (TSC), which carried the bombs side-by-side, on the weapon stations at the front and rear of each shoulder pylon doubled this total to eight, although the drag then became very high. It was also possible to fit a centre-line

pylon between the 'shoulders' to carry five bombs, but lack of space precluded carriage of this load with the twin-store carriers. Laser-guided bombs (LGB) were too long to fit in tandem on the shoulder pylons. So three were carried, one on the front of each 'shoulder' and one on the centre-line. It was

Tornado 'B-10' on the pan at RAF Cottesmore. (GMS)

also possible to carry a 1,500-litre (330-gallon) tank on the centre station of each 'shoulder'; the carrier bomb light stores (CBLS) occupied these stations when dropping practice bombs. Two Mauser 27 mm revolver cannon were fitted under the nose; these were similar to the Aden gun, but had a much higher muzzle velocity and were therefore more accurate. They had two rates of fire, the operational rate being about 1,700 rounds per minute each, while the training rate was 1,100, and 'rounds remaining' counters were fitted in the front cockpit. Stub pylons were fitted on the insides of the inboard pylons, and these carried launcher rails for AIM-9L Sidewinder missiles. The outboard pylons were not used for bombs, but the Sky Shadow ECM and BOZ chaff/flare dispenser pods were often carried on the left and right outboard pylons respectively. This was done even in training, as it reduced the wing-root bending moment, and consequently fatigue. The aircraft could therefore carry a full bomb load, two drop-tanks, ECM, chaff, flares and Sidewinder missiles simultaneously. Offensive weapon loads for the Tornado GR1 could include 1,000 lb bombs (retarded and free-fall), LGBs, the BL755 canister ballistic unit (CBU), or cluster-bombs, and the JP233. The latter was a huge device and was the primary runway and area-denial weapon. It weighed nearly five tons and comprised two pairs of large streamlined containers carrying a considerable number of runway-cratering bombs and area-denial mines. Its weight and drag certainly reduced the aircraft's speed. At the beginning of the Gulf War the air-launched anti-radar missile

(ALARM) was introduced for attacking enemy ground radars. This was carried on normal bomb pylons, or on stubs on both sides of the inboard pylons. As the Buccaneer was phased out shortly after the Gulf War, the Tornado was also adapted to carry the Sea-Eagle anti-ship missile.

The first event was lay-down, a low-level attack which was the normal way of delivering retarded bombs and CBU, and we soon moved on to toss or 'loft' bombing. I started night flying at the end of January 1989 with a dual flight to check my proficiency at circuits and landings as well as instrument approaches, after which I moved on to night range work, which really showed the Tornado's capability. On day range sorties we flew a short low-level navigation exercise to the range, practising off-range simulated attack profiles (SAP), including JP233 deliveries, *en route*. The weapon system had a 'bogus facility' which enabled the correct weapon-aiming symbology to be displayed and a simulated attack to be made, even though the JP233 was not carried. HUD symbology for the JP233 was very similar to that for the retarded 1,000 lb bomb, but with the markers showing the beginning and end of the stick of weapons, which could be up to the length of the runway being attacked.

I started my Tornado flying with II (AC) Squadron at Laarbruch in March 1989. The squadron was equipped with the Tornado GR1A, which was the reconnaissance version of the GR1, although initially they had no recce equipment fitted but carried ballast instead. Their aircraft were early GR1s with the guns and ammunition tanks removed to make way for the

new equipment, which was not yet ready. This installation had the advantage that it was internal and thus produced no additional drag or handling problems, and apart from having no guns the aircraft could still carry the same weapon load as the GR1. Because of the growing number of different weapons which were becoming available for the Tornado, squadrons were now tending to specialise on using a particular one, such as the JP233, or the LOB, although they could still fulfil the other roles if required. As II (AC) Squadron concentrated primarily on the recce role, they were stuck with the more basic weapons such as the 1,000 lb bombs and the CBU in their secondary attack role.

I received a posting to 13 Squadron, which was being re-formed with Tornadoes at Honington in Suffolk. The squadron re-formed at Honington on 1 January 1990, having originally been a Canberra reconnaissance unit, and two of the navigators already there had been with the earlier unit on Canberras. The squadron was still not fully up to strength when I arrived on 15 June, and a steady trickle of new crews continued to appear as the

Engine technicians working on the Tornado's RB199-03R engines at RAF Cottesmore. (GMS)

last few aircraft were collected from the British Aerospace airfield at Warton, in Lancashire. These were brand-new Batch 7 aircraft, with all the latest modifications incorporated. The squadron accommodation was also new and purpose-built for the recce role; the protected briefing facility (PBF) included the reconnaissance intelligence centre (RIC). Initially, only a few aircraft had the recce equipment fitted, so the CO decided to give priority to working up all crews to combat readiness in the attack role. The CO gave me an arrival check in a dual-control Tornado before I moved straight into bounced simulated attack profiles (SAPs), and I was checked out as a pair's leader within the week. On my next flight, the CO led nine aircraft in a diamond-formation flypast over the airfield to celebrate the squadron's first 1,000 hours of flying. Early in July I set off in a four-aircraft formation for a two-night stop at Aalborg, near the Northern tip of Denmark. On the second day we did a cross-country trip at 1,000 feet

An engine technician working on a Tornado RB199-03R engine at RAF Cottesmore. (GMS)

to the Tranum Range for lay-down and dive bombing in the morning, while in the afternoon the four aircraft did fighter affiliation with four Danish F-16s over the Baltic. It was a very interesting time, rushing around at low level and extremely high speed in afterburner, attempting to prevent the F-16s from getting into a firing position, although with so much use of the burner, the trip only lasted just over an hour.

Next came my introduction to air-to-air refuelling (AAR). At that time, squadrons in RAF Germany did not do AAR as they were relatively close to the front line during the Cold War. However, this situation changed with the work-up for the Gulf War later in the year. After a detailed briefing, I set off with the Squadron QFI in the rear cockpit of a dual-control GR1 to joust with a Victor. The refuelling probe on the GR1 was retractable, and was an easily fitted and removed modification on the right side of the forward fuselage; virtually all aircraft on the squadron were so equipped. The Tornado F3 had a built-in retractable probe, fitted during

Tornado 'BA' of 14 Squadron at the TTTE at RAF Cottesmore. (GMS)

A Tornado being prepared for a training flight at RAF Cottesmore. (GMS)

manufacture and stowed internally on the left side of the forward fuselage. The tankers flew in set racetrack patterns over the North Sea, and all details, including call-signs, tanker tow-line (pattern), height, radio frequencies and fuel required were co-ordinated before take-off. Approaching the tow-line, radar vectors were obtained from ground radar units, while the range from the tanker was displayed on the air-to-air Tacan indicator in the cockpit. Once the tanker was in sight, the formation leader requested permission to join up, and when cleared the formation moved up on the right side of the

tanker and slightly forward of the cockpit so that the tanker pilot could see them. Normally, the tanker flew at 280 knots at between 20,000 and 25,000 feet, and ideally it was intercepted by cutting the corners of the racetrack pattern. Frequently, however, a tail chase was required, and it then took some time to catch up, resulting in the normal tendency to approach with excessive closing speed, in which the tanker suddenly appeared to 'bloom' in size, and it was then difficult to lose speed quickly enough. The airbrakes were not very effective at low indicated airspeeds, and it was better not to use them in

A Tornado ready for taxiing at RAF Cottesmore. (GMS)

considerable amount of left rudder trim to counter. Dropping rearwards, the aircraft was then slid across behind one of the hoses trailed from each of the tanker's wing pods: in addition to the fuselage centre-line hose, both the Victor and the VC-10 had wing pods which allowed two receiver aircraft to be refuelled simultaneously. It was my first experience in close formation with a large aircraft, and they were actually quite close, as the hoses were only about sixty feet long when fully extended. Although it was not too difficult, care had to be taken, as the penalty for a mistake could be a collision. The basket on the end of the hose was like a giant shuttlecock about eighteen inches in diameter, and the QFI then took control to demonstrate how to make contact. After stabilising the Tornado about six feet behind the basket, he applied a small amount of extra power so that they were overtaking smoothly at about walking pace, tracking the rear end of the pod and not looking at the basket, until contact was made. Initially, the basket appeared low, but as the Tornado approached, the bow wave of the blunt nose of the GR1 pushed the basket up and out to provide a good contact. Excessive overtaking speed was dangerous as the probe could be pushed between the spokes of the basket. Any debris was then liable to go down the right engine intake, probably causing serious problems, while any

this situation as, if the leader was already throttled back to idle, the rest of the formation then had nothing else to use and were liable to overtake him.

Joining the tanker in good weather was not too difficult, but it could be rather tricky in poor weather, as it was necessary to keep a good look-out for other formations joining or leaving. The probe was selected out while still abeam the tanker, and this produced a noticeable increase in drag, as well as a yaw to the right which required a damage to the basket rendered it unusable for other aircraft, which could be short of fuel. Approaching too slowly could cause a 'soft contact' in which the probe was not pushed sufficiently firmly into the basket to open the refuelling valve.

Experience had shown that looking at the basket frequently caused pilots to over-control and have problems in making a

good contact. The one thing that was required for AAR was smooth flying, and anything which detracted from this was likely to cause problems, in damage either to the receiver's probe or to the basket. With more experience, I found it was possible to steal quick glances at the basket in order to assist in judging corrections. The navigator or another pilot in the

*TTTE Tornadoes on the line at RAF Cottesmore. The nearest aircraft is GT.024 43+43 of **MFG 1**. (GMS)*

*Tornado 43+10 of the **Luftwaffe** on finals. This Tornado operated as 'G-29' at the TTTE from 1983 to 1984. (GMS)*

rear cockpit also assisted with a commentary and advice during the approach. In any turbulence, the whole operation could become very tricky as the basket flailed up and down, and all the receiver pilot could do was to make a steady approach and accept the fact that he was likely to miss. Under these conditions it was easy for the pilot to become tense and to over-control on both the stick and the throttles, compounding the problems. If the receiver moved forward the hose was reeled into the pod, and it was reeled out if he moved back. Markings on the hose helped in judging the correct position, and breaking contact was simply a matter of reducing power and sliding slowly rearwards until the probe was pulled out of the basket.

Conditions were perfect, and the QFI gave a good demonstration in making contact at the first attempt and then slowly easing out for me to have a go. All went well until I made contact with the basket. Unfortunately I was about nine inches high and the probe hit the rim. Normally this caused no problem, as the probe either bounced in or out of the basket, but on this occasion it caught the fabric rim and pushed it right back. The QFI immediately took control, closed the throttles and dropped out. We then studied the basket closely: some of the spokes were bent and support wires were broken, and there was the possibility that small pieces had gone into the engine, so we went straight back to base. It was an ignominious end to my first attempt at AAR, but post-flight inspection revealed no damage to the engine; however, I had to wait a month for another chance.

Squadron training continued throughout July with a mixture of simulated attack profiles, operational low flying, recce sorties and a night-flying check: this variety was much to my liking as it maintained interest and kept the brain active. Exercise Mallet Blow lasted a week in early August. As usual, this was held mainly over the Otterburn Range in Northumberland and the Spadeadam Range, and provided a complete scenario of activities. There were attacks against targets covered by Rapier SAMs at Otterburn, using practice bombs and a number of inert retarded 1,000 lb bombs. Simulated SAMs! AAA were positioned at Spadeadam, with Dutch Patriot SAM and Flycatcher AAA radar in the Pennines, plus evasion against defending Tornado F3s, which endeavoured to intercept us _en route_ between these areas. Overall the exercise provided superb training, and I greatly enjoyed it, whether leading a four-ship formation or flying as wingman.

In mid-August I started rear-seat conversion training in the dual-control Tornado, preparing for the forthcoming Qualified Weapons Instructor (QWI) course. This opened a new aspect covering the use of the radar and navigation equipment, which was normally the province of the navigator. In the trainer the left TV tabulator (TV Tab) screen was omitted, and a number of items in the rear cockpit had been moved around to allow room for the control column, throttles and flight instrument panel on the left side. Unlike the Jaguar T2, there was no HUD, and certain controls, such as that for the undercarriage, were only in the front cockpit, so that the instructor had to ask for the pilot in the front to operate these when required. As the rear cockpit was not raised, view directly ahead was poor, although this was only a problem for low-level flying and landing. With no HUD, instrument flying was by using the head-down instruments only, and it was then necessary to apply corrections to the altimeter and airspeed indicator readings, as these were not as accurate as those in the front cockpit. I found that the nav/attack system controls were not nearly as user friendly as in the Jaguar, and it could be quite awkward to change data, particularly on the TV Tab keys. Using the radar was a completely new experience and a bit of a black art as far as I was concerned, but I soon grasped the basics and was able to mark larger features and offsets on IP to target runs. However, I realised that I would never develop the skills of a professional navigator, who could identify remarkably small features, in the limited time available. The initial trips were simply to get used to flying from the rear cockpit, especially for landing and operating the navigation and attack equipment. On the range we practised the various modes of attack, and I found that I was kept busy with operating all the weapons, as the majority of attack modes were controlled from the rear cockpit. Some of the attack modes took several switch selections, where I considered that a couple would have sufficed with better system design. Overall I enjoyed flying from the rear cockpit as it enabled me to see the navigator's task in the Tornado. The fourth and final trip was a check ride with a senior QFI from the Tornado Weapons Conversion Unit Standards Flight; all went well and I passed.

Later in August it was back to AAR, and I did four consecutive sorties. The first was in a dual-control aircraft on a VC-10 tanker. This time everything went smoothly and I made contacts with both wing hoses and that on the centre-line. The centre-line hose was slightly larger and heavier than the wing hoses, and different reference points were used when making contact. For some reason which I never really understood it was considered to be slightly more difficult making contact on the centre-line than on the wing hoses. The initial contact attempts included a couple of misses, and these were all planned to be 'dry', with no fuel passed from the tanker. Once I had mastered the procedure, we moved on to 'wet' contacts. For these the tanker crew made the necessary switch selections so that fuel was passed when a firm contact had opened the refuelling valves in the hose drum unit. Red, amber and green lights controlled from the tanker flight deck were mounted adjacent to each hose drum unit and gave the following indications: Red – keep clear or break away if in contact; Amber – clear to approach for contact; Green – with the receiver probe locked into the basket, the hose has wound in far enough to open the fuel valves. I took on about 500 gallons (two tons) of fuel on one of the contacts, and it was noticeable that more power was required to maintain position as aircraft weight and drag increased, until finally I was at maximum dry power. As weight increased further, it was necessary to select the afterburner on one engine and adjust the power on the other, until modulated afterburner power had to be used on the second engine. Small throttle movements caused large changes of thrust when afterburner

A German student pilot and his instructor deplane from Tornado IDS 44+74 after a training flight at RAF Cottesmore. This aircraft served with JBG 32 at Lechfeld in October 1985 and JBG 33 at Buchel in 1986. (GMS)

was in use, and it was therefore necessary to avoid over-controlling on the throttles. We were supposed to break AAR contact before selecting afterburner, but apparently no one did. Fuel was transferred at the rate of about 200 gallons per minute at maximum flow.

An AAR trip against a TriStar tanker came next, carrying an experienced navigator who was also an AAR instructor (AARI). The TriStar had no wing hoses, but two were fitted on the centre-line, only one of which could be deployed at any one time, the second being a reserve in case of problems with

II (AC) Squadron's Tornado GR1s after arrival at Marham in December 1991. (RAF Marham)

the first. Although it carried a tremendous amount of fuel, the ability to refuel only one aircraft at a time was a significant limitation. Close up, the TriStar appeared to be as big as a block of flats, and it had the reputation of being the most difficult of tankers for making successful contacts. When in contact, the Tornado was under the TriStar's tail, and care had to be taken not to get too high, otherwise the fin entered the jet wash from the tanker's centre engine, which was felt as a vibration through the airframe. In the event, it took me only a couple of attempts to make a successful contact, and I then took on a full load of fuel before embarking on a recce trip, which terminated with a visit to a weapons range. The total flying time for this trip was two hours and twenty-five minutes.

Two more AA trips were made with navigator AARIs – the first against a Victor and the second on a TriStar. Apart from the fact that it carried much less fuel, the refuelling characteristics for the Victor were very similar to those of the VC-10. Having completed four successful AAR conversion trips by day, I was now cleared to carry out the exercise with my own navigator in the rear cockpit. The next trip was my fifth consecutive AAR sortie, but this time I was in a formation for a pairs-attack sortie on a range. Without AAR, a typical recce sortie from Honington, which is in the middle of East Anglia, was to fly at medium level to let down abeam Harrogate and then at low level across the Pennines to the

western side of the UK. The route then either turned north through the Lake District or passed to the east of the Lakes, crossing the Spadeadam Range for a west–east run across southern Scotland, passing south of Glasgow and Edinburgh, before turning south down the eastern side of the Pennines. A First Run Attack was then carried out on one of the ranges near the Humber, or in the Wash. If fuel permitted, a couple of further passes were made on the range before pulling away with minimum fuel for the return to base. When AAR was available, the sortie was normally programmed to climb to medium level over the North Sea to the tanker towline and fly north of Newcastle before letting down to low level. With the extra fuel, it was then possible to route up into central Scotland, and this extended the flight time with a standard 7.4 tons of fuel load from an hour and three-quarters to about two and a half hours.

The rest of August was taken up with mixed training, mainly operational low flying (OLF) with fighter affiliation. For the last trips of the month I did OLF in Scotland, landing at Leuchars in the afternoon, followed by a night low-level parallel-track-formation attack sortie on the return to Honington. This was to be my last trip on the squadron before starting the QWI course, although this only involved a minor move to the Tornado Weapons Conversion Unit on the far side of the airfield. August had been a good month, with mixed and interesting flying in which AAR had helped to bring my

GR1A ZA398/S of II (AC) Squadron, GR1 'JM' of 27 Squadron and GR1 'X' of 617 Squadron with Victor K.2 XH672 Maid Marian of 55 Squadron in 1993. (RAF Marham)

A GR1A in a hardened aircraft shelter (HAS). (RAF Marham)

GR1A 'FB' of 13 Squadron in a hardened aircraft shelter (HAS) at RAF Marham in July 1993. (Author)

total to over thirty-seven hours' flying. The aircraft on 13 Squadron enjoyed noticeably better serviceability than those on other squadrons as they were brand-new and incorporated all the modifications designed to improve reliability, and the squadron also had very good engineers.

On 2 August 1990 Iraq had invaded Kuwait, and the coalition of Western and Arab nations began to build up their military strength in the Middle East to counter this aggression. On 9 August the MoD announced the dispatch of a dozen each of Tornado F.3 air-defence fighters and Jaguar GR1A attack aircraft to the Gulf. Operation *Granby*, the British contribution to *Desert Shield/Desert Storm* to liberate Kuwait, had begun. No. 29 (F) Squadron's F3s were already half-way deployed in Cyprus for an armament practice camp (APC) and had been joined at RAF Akrotiri by 5 Squadron, which was about to start its APC. No. 29 Squadron was preparing to return to the UK when a signal was received 'to remain in theatre'. On 11 August twelve F3s and crews of Nos 29 and 5 Squadrons flew to Dhahran, in Saudi Arabia, and the remaining aircrew and ground crew flew out by Hercules. By 12 August the twelve F3s were available at Dhahran with twenty-two crews, supported by over 200 ground crew. The first F3 combat air patrol (CAP) was flown on 12 August, just south of the Kuwait–Saudi border. Later, the MoD produced its first 'roulement', and the detachment was replaced by Tornadoes from RAF Leeming, which were by now equipped with the superior Stage 1 Plus Operation *Granby* F3s. All

A JP233 being loaded under the fuselage of a Tornado. (RAF Marham)

the RAF's refuelling assets were needed to deliver the Tornado GR1s, F3s and Jaguars in the UK and Europe to Tabuk and Dhahran and the former RAF Muharraq, now Bahrain International Airport. In August and September the dispatch of Tornado GR1 squadrons at Brüggen and Laarbruch in RAF Germany to Bahrain, Saudi Arabia and Dhahran began. All the GR1s were painted in hastily applied 'Desert Pink' camouflage. A further eighteen GR1s were sent to the region in January 1991 to complement the Tornado F3s. All the Tornado GR1/1As deployed to the Gulf were from RAF Germany, including even those held in reserve at Marham, as these were powered with the more powerful Mk 103 version of the RB199 turbofan.

In the meantime, Kevin Noble happily proceeded on his QWI course; unaware of what effect these events would have on his future career. On the course he practised medium-level bombing and 45° dive-bombing. Medium-level bombing was relatively easy for the pilot, and could even be done on autopilot. The navigator marked the target on his radar screen and the pilot simply followed his directions.

It was not terribly accurate as the aircraft could only measure the velocity of the wind in which it was flying, and the direction and strength could vary greatly at lower altitudes. From 20,000 feet, free-fall bombs took over 40 seconds to reach the ground, and the wind could affect their trajectory significantly in that time. Dive-bombing at 45° was great fun, but the workload was very high and it was not easy to obtain good results. Again, the navigator marked the target on his screen and the pilot made the initial weapons-switch selections as they approached the free-fall release point. Then, at the 'moment critique', the pilot rolled the aircraft inverted and pulled down to point at the target in an inverted 45° dive. He then rolled the right way up and made the necessary

A Tornado dispensing its JP233 clusters of anti-personnel mines from the front, and retarded runway-cratering bomblets from the rear section. (BAe)

corrections to get the HUD bomb-fall line onto the target, simultaneously making the final switch selections and controlling the weapon-aiming system on his hand controller. Meanwhile speed increased rapidly, and having got everything sorted out, the pilot pressed the 'commit' button. The bomb was released by the computer at the calculated point shortly thereafter. The pilot then pulled out of the dive and into a climb for another go if on the range, or to get away from the enemy defences if on operations, simultaneously making the weapons switches safe.

Steep dive-bombing was quite accurate – about the same as low-level bombing – but it required clear weather to enable the pilot to see the target, and the aircraft came much closer to the ground and therefore within range of AAA and short-range SAMs. Dive-toss bombing involved the aircraft entering a 20° dive before pulling out at the correct altitude (about

Desert-Pink-painted Tornado GR1s 'EE' and 'Q' and ZA471/E Emma in the foreground during the Gulf War. (Air Commodore Ian MacFadyen)

F3 ZE159/DO on CAP over the Gulf. (MoD)

2,500 feet) and range from the target, the bomb being released as the dive angle reduced through about 10°. Weapons sorties onto ranges were made as realistic as possible by including fighter affiliation with Tornado F3s and Sea Harriers. Even with a combat load of four inert 1,000 lb bombs, the Tornado still handled and performed well and the extra weight was hardly noticeable. The return to base was made via the Tam Range in the Moray Firth, where two retarded bombs were released in a stick lay-down attack on a line of tank hulks, and this was followed by a stick loft release against another target.

On the afternoon of 16 January 1991 Operation *Desert Storm* began. The Coalition had built an air force of 2,790 aircraft, over half of which were combat aircraft. Included in this total was the RAF contribution of 135 aircraft, which included forty-six Tornado GR1/1A attack and reconnaissance aircraft. The initial requirement from RAF Strike Command was that the six Victor tankers in theatre should support the Tornado F.3 and Jaguar missions only and the VC 10 detachment would support all Tornado sorties. At one minute after midnight on 17 January 1991, active service was declared for all British personnel in the Gulf theatre of operation. After intensive training and a considerable period of '48 hours notice to go', 43 (F) Squadron's F3s had arrived at Dhahran in the early hours of Saturday 1 December 1990 to join Saudi, US and French fighters in the air defence of Saudi Arabia. The first crews were flying F3s on CAPs by the morning of the next day, providing both air defence of Saudi Arabia from the Iraqi bomber threat and protection of the many reconnaissance and AWACs aircraft from possible fighter attack. Covering these high-value assets remained

a task throughout the hostilities, but as the land war approached the F3s were also given the job of covering RAF attack aircraft should they be bounced by Iraqi fighters over the area of the land battle. The F3s were an integral part of an air-defence system which included surface-to-air missiles, airborne and ground radars, guns of various calibres and the fighter aircraft of the Coalition. The F3 CAPs were placed as barriers just south of the Saudi–Kuwait border. These CAPs were usually manned for twenty-four hours a day by the crews of 43 and also 29 Squadron, which had arrived in mid-December to make up the second half of the 'composite' squadron. An extensive work-up programme had been completed by the crews in the UK. This included AR5 flying, combat to reduced base heights and a thorough night vision goggles (NVG) flying phase. The crews also felt at home with the improved Stage 1 Plus F3s, and had studied the capabilities of the enemy.

On 16 January two Victors led the first Muharraq Tornado GR1 bombing mission into Iraq. In the first week of January the twelve Tornado crews of 14 Squadron, who had the most theatre experience, went home and were replaced by six from 27 Squadron and six from 617 Squadron. XV Squadron plus attrition reserves from IX (B) Squadron made up the rest of the Muharraq detachment. XV Squadron crews flew in two waves of four. The target for the eight Tornadoes was Al Tallil, a huge airfield twice the size of Heathrow, in south Iraq, north-west of Basrah. The Tornado crews were to cut the two 11,000 ft parallel runways and the access taxiways leading from the hardened aircraft shelters (HAS) with JP233 anti-airfield weapons. All eight Tornadoes refuelled successfully at around 15,000 feet, and about one hour and twenty minutes after take-off they left the tankers and headed north. They descended to 500 feet and then went down to 200 feet as they approached the target area. Support packages of fighter sweep 'Wild Weasels' and jammers and F-15s confirmed that they too were on time. The American package of about thirty aircraft was going to the same target and would bomb from around 20,000 feet. The Tornadoes bombed one minute after them so that their JP233 minefield would be undisturbed. Despite Triple-A and SAMs, all eight delivered their JP233s at low level and cleared the target at 550 knots. The Tornadoes arrived safely back at Muharraq four hours and five minutes after take-off, to an enthusiastic welcome. The next wave, to Ar Rumaylah airfield for daylight lofting or 'toss-bombing' of 1,000-pounders, also went ahead without loss, and post-strike photos showed a very successful outcome and no more than a twenty-foot error. Over the next three days the Muharraq detachment was to lose three Tornado crews in quick succession. One of ZD791's AIM-9L Sidewinders was hit by flak, exploded and 'took out' the engine, forcing Flight Lieutenants John Peters (26) and Adrian 'John' Nichol (27) of XV Squadron to eject. They were captured by the Iraqis and endured a brutal imprisonment before their release on 4 March 1991.

On the night of 17/18 January a four-ship Tornado attack was made on Ubaydah bin al Jarrah airfield, and another four on Al Tallil airfield. Each of the eight Tornadoes was loaded with two JP233s. One Tornado suffered a bird strike that removed a large section of the port wing's leading edge. The Tornado was immediately patched and flown back to Brüggen for repair. Three days later it was redelivered to the Gulf and went on to complete thirty-five missions. ZA392, flown by 27 Squadron's 39-year-old CO, Wing Commander Nigel Elsdon, and his 42-year-old navigator, Flight Lieutenant Robert 'Max' Collier, was hit three minutes after 'bombs away' and crashed into the ground, killing both crew. There was now an unspoken fear about who was going to be next.

On 18 January two Dhahran F3s committed north into occupied Kuwait. A formation of American A-10 attack aircraft was escaping south and being chased by Iraqi fighters. The F3s moved at high speed, blowing off their fuel drop-tanks and locking their targets from long range with the Foxhunter radars. The targets, no doubt fully aware of the approaching Tornadoes from their own radar warning alarms and their ground control radar operators, turned tail and ran north. On various other occasions the Tornadoes of both 43 and 29 committed north into Iraq and Kuwait, and came under fire from Iraqi-operated defence systems, most notably 57 mm and 23 mm AAA guns. However, after a few fighter air-defence sorties by Fulcrum and Mirage Fl aircraft, the Iraqi Air Force played no more part in the war. There were no enemy offensive bombing operations, but the F3s continued to wait on the border and were used in the early days when the Iraqis still flew.

The Tornado GR1 crews were flying night-combat sorties only, and at Muharraq on 19/20 January eight attacked Al Tallil airbase. Four of the Tornadoes were armed with JP233s and another four were loaded with eight 1,000-pounders fused for an airburst fifteen feet above the Iraqi gun emplacements. Seven Tornadoes (the eighth developed mechanical failure) reached the target, where GR1 ZA396, crewed by Flight Lieutenant David Waddington and his 44-year-old navigator, Flight Lieutenant Robert Stewart, who was also from 27 Squadron, was shot down by a Euromissile Roland SAM. Both men survived ejection and were captured. They were repatriated after the end of the war. The JP233 attacks were

An F3 of 111 (F) Squadron armed with AIM-9L Sidewinders. In its usual air-defence role the F3 can receive real-time information on approaching targets via a datalink from patrolling AEW Sentry aircraft and attack nominated targets using AMRAAM missiles. (MoD)

changed to medium level after the night of 20 January. By 23 January five Tornadoes had been lost in action. Though the Tornado force represented just 4% of the Coalition air strength, it had suffered 26% of the casualties. It was obvious to all that precision-guided weapons were the only salvation if the Tornadoes were to remain at medium level.

Ferranti (later GEC Ferranti) had been involved in the development of a laser designator for use with laser-guided bombs (LGBs) since 1973. This culminated in the production of a thermal imaging airborne laser designator (TIALD) pod which had been under flight development on a Buccaneer at RAE Farnborough since early 1988. Buccaneers fitted with the Pavespike pod, which provided a manually controlled TV picture by day only, were deployed to Bahrain and Dhahran to act as laser designators for the Tornadoes to direct their LGBs on to their targets. Between 10 and 27 February seventy-two successful TIALD sorties were flown and twenty-three were aborted. A total of 218 Buccaneer/Tornado missions were flown and twenty-four bridges and fifteen airfields were attacked, during which 169 LGBs were dropped (forty-eight by Buccaneers). What was needed urgently was a laser designator for use on the Tornado to direct LGBs onto the target at night. A terrific effort was made to bring forward a prototype laser designator for use on the Tornado.

To permit day-and-night operation under varying weather conditions, TIALD was equipped with thermal imaging and a TV camera, which were mounted in a pod carried beneath the aircraft.

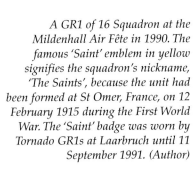

A GR1 of 16 Squadron at the Mildenhall Air Fête in 1990. The famous 'Saint' emblem in yellow signifies the squadron's nickname, 'The Saints', because the unit had been formed at St Omer, France, on 12 February 1915 during the First World War. The 'Saint' badge was worn by Tornado GR1s at Laarbruch until 11 September 1991. (Author)

F3 ZE167/AL of 65 Squadron (Shadow for 229 OCU – note the quiver and torch on the fin) getting airborne at the Mildenhall Air Fête in 1987. (Author)

The designator was integrated into the aircraft's navigation and attack (nav/attack) system to enable it to be directed and controlled, and the thermal or visual images were recorded by the infra-red recce recorder in the Tornado GR1A. Arrival of the TIALD-equipped Tornadoes allowed Tabuk to switch to precision missions on 30 February, and from then until the end of the Gulf War the Tornadoes at all three bases flew few free-fall-bombing missions. Initially only four GR1 crews from 13 Squadron had received training on TIALD equipment at Boscombe Down, but once in the Gulf, one crew from II (AC) Squadron and another from 14 Squadron were trained. Two crews from 16 Squadron and three crews plus the CO of 617 Squadron had also been trained. Starting

on 8 February 1991, a total of ninety-five TIALD missions were carried out in the nineteen days up to the cease-fire, 261 LGBs hit their targets and no aircraft were lost. The TIALD aircraft were supported by a total of fourteen Tornado GR1 bombers. Throughout this period, only the two original TIALD pods, which had been built for development purposes, were available, and these were shuffled between a maximum of five Tornado GR1s, which had received the necessary modifications to accept them. In use these two pods had proved to be both reliable and user friendly. One pod registered 100% serviceability and the other 98.2%.

Flight Lieutenant Kevin Noble flew eleven TIALD sorties with Jerry Cass. No. 13 Squadron had been selected to introduce TIALD

F3 ZD932/AM of 229 OCU at RAF Coningsby landing at the Mildenhall Air Fête in 1985. This aircraft first flew on 22 March 1985. (Author)

into service, and they were one of four experienced crews that had been nominated to carry out development trials at Boscombe Down. Five aircraft were modified at Honington with the necessary wiring to link the main computer and the system control panel in the rear cockpit with the front of the left shoulder pylon, where the TIALD pod was to be mounted. The aircraft also had the other special modifications required by all Operation *Granby* aircraft. These included the Have Quick frequency-hopping, anti-jamming radio and the Mode IV Identification Friend or Foe (IFF) equipment for compatibility with that used by the US forces and their airborne warning and control system (AWACs) aircraft. All engines had to be fitted with single crystal turbine blades, as early experience in the desert revealed problems with sand melting on the original blades and blocking their cooling-air ducts.

The normal procedure was for two bomber aircraft to fly at about 20,000 feet in close proximity to the Tornado, which carried the TIALD pod but no bombs: this allowed two sticks of bombs to be dropped on two targets in a single pass by the TIALD aircraft. Each of the bombers carried a maximum of three LGBs. On the run-up, the TIALD aircraft fired its laser designator for a period of about thirty seconds to illuminate the target. The laser energy was reflected back over a large area in the general direction of the designator. Within these reflections was a region in the form of an inverted cone known as the 'basket' (not to be confused with the AAR basket). It was necessary for the bomber aircraft to drop their bombs within this 'basket' if the laser seeker in the nose of the bomb was to receive signals of sufficient energy to acquire the target. It was also necessary for the canard control fins and tail wings to be able to deflect the bomb onto it from its normal trajectory. As soon as the bombs were observed to burst on the first target, the designator was aligned on the second target and fired to guide the bombs, which had already been released, from the second aircraft. Later, with experience, it became possible for the TIALD aircraft to designate four targets in a single pass.

Kevin Noble's and Jerry Cass's first TIALD mission was on 8 February, against an airfield in western Iraq known as H3 North West, which was near the Jordanian border The first two bombers thundered off into the night at thirty-second intervals, with their twin blue afterburner flames fading into the distance as they accelerated. These then disappeared as the burners were cancelled, leaving only the flashing navigation lights visible; meanwhile Kevin counted down the seconds on the stopwatch, before taking off in

A GR1 of 617 'Dam Busters' Squadron taking off at RAF Marham. (Author)

A GR1 of 617 'Dam Busters' Squadron taking off at RAF Marham. (Author)

pursuit. They climbed up to level out at just above 20,000 feet, checking with the duty AWACs as they left Tabuk, and he then gave regular reports of 'picture clear', meaning that there were no enemy fighters airborne. It was a fine clear night, and all the formation was in sight as they climbed. After about thirty minutes they were approaching the Iraqi border and completed the 'fence checks' before entering enemy airspace: these included arming the guns and AIM-9 Sidewinder missiles and switching all external lights out. Everything was going smoothly, the aircraft was fully serviceable and the formation was in good shape and on time. Below it was completely dark, as there was no habitation in the desert. Soon after crossing the border, they saw bomb flashes some miles to the east as another target was attacked, and these were immediately followed by the first sight of AAA. This consisted of dense, multi-coloured white, red and blue flashes, and was fairly typical in that the defences only opened fire after the first bombs had landed. However, it all seemed to explode well below them, so AAA did not appear to present much of a threat at medium level.

Meanwhile [recalls Kevin Noble] Jerry was giving a good confidence-building commentary from the navigation system. He had identified all the fixes accurately on radar, the TIALD pod was working properly and he was also able to track other aircraft ahead on the radar. The radar homing and warning receiver (RHWR) remained pretty quiet throughout, with mainly friendly fighter indications, although a couple of short-duration strobes from enemy SAM systems appeared. Chaff was dropped and we manoeuvred, looking for the threat, but nothing was seen so we continued on our way. Apparently a

A line-up of **Luftwaffe** *Tornadoes at Marham in July 1996. The nearest aircraft is G-71 43+13 GS002. (Author)*

F3 ZG774/WK of 56 (R) Squadron at RAF Leuchars in the famous 'Firebirds' display scheme at RAF Coltishall on 19 September 2005. (Author)

long streak of rocket flame indicated that the SAM was not heading for us: however, a wobbling red dot would show that it was coming our way and it was time to take drastic action.

Soon we were approaching the target, and Jerry identified the airfield from over twenty miles away, zooming in on the TIALD to the north-west corner for the first hardened aircraft shelter (HAS). All went smoothly as we approached and went through the pre-planned procedures in preparation for the attack. These culminated in the first bomber releasing his load of three LGBs on time. Meanwhile we were already in the turn to fly past the airfield, following our own route to one side of and above the bomber. We flew high as we were lighter than the bombers and also did not wish to have bombs whistling past our ears in the darkness. As the first bomber called 'bombs gone', I started my stopwatch to give Jerry the count-down. By this time, Jerry was tracking the side of the target HAS and fired the laser for the last part of the bombs' flight while I then gave the count-down to impact, which was forty seconds after release. As the count reached zero, Jerry called 'Splash', as he saw the bombs impact on his TV Tab screen. But there was no time to waste since the second stick of LGBs was already in the air. Jerry zoomed out on the TIALD pod viewing head and 'walked' the tracking cross out of the HAS site, down the runway, up the fourth taxiway to the HAS at the end, and zoomed in again to commence tracking. All this only took about five seconds and was done from memory – there was no time to study maps at this stage. Meanwhile I continued the count-down to the next impact, calling every

GR4 'P' of IX (B) Squadron at RAF Marham in flight. (MoD)

ten seconds, and cross-checked with Jerry that he had started firing the laser at the correct time. As Jerry was concentrating on his equipment, I looked down towards the target as best I could, while monitoring the RHWR and taking care not to dip a wing or drop-tank in the way of the TIALD's view of the target. All was quiet and the AAA was silent. Again, as I reached zero on the second ten-second count-down, Jerry saw the bombs impact on the target before zooming out to look back at the airfield to obtain good video coverage for bomb-damage assessment. By this stage we were a couple of miles beyond the target on the way out, so the pod was looking back at quite an angle. As we were departing, with our two bombers somewhere out there in the dark, we could hear the second phase of the attack going in behind as the next two bombers and TIALD aircraft went through. Soon, they too were pulling out behind us, and our bombers and we were all heading for home.

As we crossed back into Saudi airspace, I made the weapons switches safe and turned the navigation lights on; many other lights also appeared up and down the border as various other aircraft crossed out of Iraq. For some reason, the crews often referred to Iraq as 'sausage side', but the origin of this appellation is not known. The return to base was uneventful and we were soon in the stream of aircraft landing at Tabuk. I felt great elation and relief that everything had gone according to plan, and the results for our formation appeared to be good. This first operational mission into Iraq had been successful and we had all returned: it was a big hurdle to have crossed and we now knew roughly what to expect in the future. The whole trip had only lasted an hour and forty minutes, so it was a relatively short introduction to operations. It was pleasant to climb out of the aircraft into the cool night air of the desert, and having signed in on the aircraft servicing documents, we gathered back at Operations for the 'hot debrief' on the mission. This was quite short and provided the first intelligence information on the success of the mission and of any threats encountered. The detachment commander was there to meet us as we came in and he remained for the debriefing, as he did on most subsequent

occasions. Then came the item we had all been waiting for – the showing of the aircraft video tapes to see how the attack had gone. This provided a great change for the bomber crews following the earlier frustration of dropping dumb bombs into the darkness: we could now actually see where the bombs had gone. On the videos from both TIALDs it was just possible to see the bombs as dots sliding across the screen to hit the big earth-covered HAS in a great hot flash which showed up well on the IR picture, the blast shooting out from both ends of the HAS. The mission was definitely successful.

The second trip was very similar to the first, the target being HAS on H2, another airfield in western Iraq. By now, experience had shown that dropping three LGBs on a HAS was wasteful and two were found to be sufficient. The HAS on this airfield were bare concrete, like their NATO counterparts, and as bombs impacted through the roof the massive doors, weighing several tons, were blasted away at great speed. Anything inside would have been completely destroyed, with aircraft inside being barely recognisable.

Our third mission targeted the runway at Mudaysis, just over a hundred miles west of Baghdad. For maximum effect, the bombs were aimed to hit the junction where the taxiways joined the runway. The attack went well except that the second set of bombs failed to detonate – they were seen to hit the runway in a small hot flash under the TIALD cross-hairs, but this was far too small to be bombs exploding, and it was very disappointing. Our fourth operational mission was our first day sortie, and was against more HAS, this time on the

A Tornado pulling in for refuelling. (MoD)

A pair of Tornadoes taking off from RAF Marham. (Author)

A Tornado pulls in to refuel from a TriStar KC1 tanker. (Tony Paxton)

A TriStar KC1 aerial tanker and four Tornado ADVs in flight. (MoD)

ADV F3 ZE862 in company with a Boeing Sentry AEW1 (E-3D). (MoD)

airfield at Jalibah South East in south-eastern Iraq, near the border with Kuwait. A large sandstorm covered the whole area, and when we arrived over Jalibah, cloud prevented the TIALD seeing the target area, so the attack was called off and we headed back to base feeling somewhat dejected. The fifth mission came on 17 February: this time it was a night sortie against the Ar Ramadi highway bridge approximately seventy miles west of Baghdad. This was our first bridge, and it carried dual carriageways over a river. At take-off I could not get one of the afterburners to light on the runway. The engine 'war rating' switch was wired in the rear position, so I moved it forward to get extra power from that engine without the afterburner, and by selecting 'combat' I raised the turbine temperatures still further to increase power. With full afterburner on the good engine, the take-off roll was rather longer than normal, but otherwise it was satisfactory. The route took us to the north of the target before turning south onto the attack heading. This time we were designating for the second pair of bombers, so Jerry could see the hot area on the bridge from the first pair's attack. There was some AAA over the target as the bombers knocked down one side of the dual carriageway, but the other side remained standing. The return to base was uneventful until I selected flaps on a long final approach – the slats came down but the flaps did not, so I left the circuit to sort out the problem. When I was still unable to lower the flaps, I elected to carry out a landing with both slats and flaps retracted, as detailed in the Emergency Procedures, as this was safer than with slats down but no flaps. I then

dumped fuel to reduce the aircraft's weight and landing speed to a minimum. Even so, the calculated speed at the runway threshold was 190 knots – about forty knots faster than normal – but the extra speed only became apparent at touch-down, when it was very noticeable. It then seemed to take ages to slow down, using reverse thrust and brakes. However, I had dealt competently with what could have been a difficult situation and the aircraft was not damaged. Initially the engineers rectified both problems, but although there were no further difficulties with the flaps, that engine was later to give trouble. The same afterburner problem subsequently happened on a number of occasions until finally a pilot was approaching the tanker for AAR about twenty minutes after take-off when his wingman reported white sparks spitting from the exhaust. These were turbine blades, which had obviously had enough of being subjected to very high temperatures. A loss of thrust, followed by the appearance of an engine vibration warning caption, caused the aircraft to slow down and start to lose height, so the pilot jettisoned tanks and returned to base. An engine change was then required, and this cured the problem.

We did our sixth mission on 19 February. This was our second in daylight and was against the Bin Al Jarrah airfield, approximately seventy miles south-east of Baghdad. The second TIALD aircraft became unserviceable, and so, as before, Jerry and I reverted to the back-up plan to designate for both pairs of bombers. It was a beautifully clear day as we approached for the attack around mid-morning, and for a change I could see the target area during the run-up. The first pair of targets were large, earth-covered, semi-buried fuel tanks. Unfortunately both bombers misidentified the offsets on the radars and released the bombs outside the basket. This was a good demonstration of why the TIALD crew needed to count down accurately, as when the count got to forty-five seconds we knew that the bombs must have landed – even though Jerry could not see them on his screen. However, we then had to leave the first target and move to the second without delay, where the same thing happened again. This was very disappointing, but Jerry and I had to put this out of our minds as we had to make a second run to pick up the following pair of bombers – the targets were large concrete ammunition bunkers to the south of the airfield. On the run-in the distinctive 'wah-wah-wah' of the RHWR was heard, plus guidance indications for the SA-3 SAM missile system, so Jerry immediately dispensed chaff while I took evasive active and scanned the sky. However, the indications ceased and nothing was seen, so we continued the run. This happened another couple of times during the attack, but the warnings were only of short duration of a second or so. The first bombs hit the target with a moderate flash on the TV screen and Jerry moved the designator on to the next bunker, but the second strike was altogether more impressive. There was an exclamation from Jerry as a huge fireball filled his screen, and after rolling out on the escape heading, I dipped a wing to look at the target. A huge mushroom cloud, resembling that from a nuclear weapon, was rising: it was very spectacular and could still be seen from eighty miles away on the way home, and by that time the smoke cloud had reached a height of about 15,000 feet.

Our seventh mission took place on 20 February, and this was to attack the runways at the former RAF base at Shaibah, just north of the Kuwaiti border, a three-hour round trip with much of the time spent over Iraq. However, it was safer to spend longer over the quiet regions of Iraq than take the shorter route near the 'hot area' of Kuwait. Patchy cloud made it difficult for Jerry to acquire the target, but eventually he got the TIALD locked on, and the bombs struck home. On the way back we had to do a night AAR. Joining the tanker was quite exciting because, as usual, there was a myriad of lights from aircraft coming out of Iraq, and several of these were visible in the tanker stack. Initially it was difficult to tell which was our tanker until we got closer and were able to identify the correct one since it was at the briefed height. It was a VC 10, and we made contact without difficulty before going home. This was to be our last trip on night operations.

On 22 February, for our eighth mission we went back to the airfield at Bin Al Jarrah, again by day, but this time we attacked the runways, and the mission was successful. For our ninth mission the following day the target was the runway at Ghalaysan, which was directly south of Baghdad, but only about seventy miles in from the Saudi border one of our bombers became unserviceable, so we only had to designate for a single aircraft. The attack was in the late afternoon, the weather was pretty poor and we were the third wave tasked

GR1s of XV (R) OCU at RAF Lossiemouth, with 'TU' nearest the camera. (MoD)

against this airfield that day. All the others had aborted because of bad weather, but Jerry and I were lucky. Having flown past large thunderstorms on the way in we initially thought that we also would fail. Luckily, as we approached there was a gap in the weather, just enough to see the target. This time we were second to designate, and I saw the bombs from the leading pair exploding on the runway; meanwhile Jerry had directed the TIALD onto their part of the runway and saw the bombs from their single bomber strike home.

The land offensive by the Allied Armies started early on the morning of 24 February. As the ground war started and the coalition tanks rolled north, the Tornado F3 CAP positions moved north with them. By Day Four of the ground war the F3s were 'capping' over Kuwait City itself and the crews were able to see clearly the results of the 'scorched-earth' policy carried out by the retreating Iraqis. The country below was littered with burning oil-well heads, polluting the skies over the whole region. Just north of the city the F3s overflew the scene of a large tank battle, where the main escape road into Iraq was littered with burnt-out equipment.

On 25 February, the target for Kevin Noble's and Jerry Cass's tenth mission was the railway bridge at Samawah, approximately

A GR1B of 12 (B) Squadron armed with Sea-Eagle stand-off anti-ship missiles on dedicated launchers under the fuselage, and the Marconi Sky Shadow ECM and BOZ-107 chaff/flare dispenser pods on the left and right outboard pylons respectively. (MoD)

120 miles south-east of Baghdad, and only about fifty miles from the Iranian border. The bombers tanked on the way to the target, but with less weight the TIALD aircraft carried a third tank on the right shoulder pylon and did not need to refuel. However, to reduce drag, the third tank, when empty, was jettisoned over Iraq, and they later estimated that it might have been over the French-held sector.

This was the only drop-tank that I ever jettisoned. Again the weather was poor, with much cloud and rain, but we met up with the bombers precisely on time before entering Iraq. The weather continued to be terrible all the way to the target. As we had been briefed that there were probably only light defences and the RHWR was quiet on approaching the area, we let down to 8,000 feet in an attempt to see the ground or the target. We found only torrential rain and could not see anything, so we aborted the mission and climbed back up for an uneventful return to base. The round trip had taken two hours and forty minutes and was a complete anti-climax, as we had achieved nothing.

Our eleventh and final mission came on the morning of 27 February, although at the time we did not know it. The targets were the fuel storage installations at Al Asad airfield, which was approximately 150 miles north-west of Baghdad. It was a crystal-clear morning after the rains: the wadis were wet and showed up darkly, looking like the veins of a leaf, while the surrounding desert was dry and light in colour. *En route*, a few blackened and burned-out targets, including an oil refinery, appeared. Our targets were large, semi-buried fuel tanks on the airfield, and good hits were obtained on both, but the strikes were not as spectacular as we had expected and certainly did not compare with the ammunition store at Bin Al Jarrah. The return to base was uneventful.

The end of the war came suddenly and unexpectedly when a cease-fire was declared on 28 February 1991. Following the expiry of the United Nations ultimatum for Iraq to withdraw from Kuwait by 15 January, air operations had started on 17 January and had continued for a total of forty-two days, while the ground war – starting on 24 February – had lasted only for a hundred hours. However, these operations resulted in the complete defeat of the Iraqi forces. Following the end of the war and in accordance with the pledge given to the Arab partners in the Coalition, which allowed for no long-term presence in the Gulf, 43 (F) and 29 (F) Squadrons withdrew as soon as both the capabilities and intentions of Iraq became clear. The Dhahran F3 detachment finished flying on 8 March 1991.

Nos 23 and 29 Squadrons have since disbanded, and the remaining F3s have had several updates. The Stage 1 upgrade included 'hands on throttle and stick' (HOTAS) controls, RAM coating and flare dispensers, while Stage 2 enhances the computer and radar imagery and adds the JTIDS data-link. The Eurofighter Typhoon is intended first to replace the F3, but as an interim measure the RAF has further upgraded a hundred F3s through a capability sustainment programme which adds a limited advanced medium-range air-to-air missile (AMRAAM) and advanced short-range air-to-air missile (ASRAAM) capability, a multiple-target engagement capability for the radar and improved defensive aids. In the months before the 2003 Gulf War, a small number of F3s underwent a modification programme to allow them to operate in the suppression of enemy air defences (SEAD) role. The modifications permitted the carriage of a pair of air-launched anti-radiation missiles (ALARM) designed to destroy or suppress the use of enemy ground-based air-defence radar systems, in place of the Sky Flash or AMRAAM missiles. In the event, the modified aircraft were not deployed during the conflict. ALARM first saw service during the Gulf War of 1991 and has been in the weapon inventory of the Tornado ever since, including the GR4 variant. The common operational value (COV) modification featured some structural rework, an NVG-compatible cockpit with new displays, GPS and Have Quick secure radios. The first CSP/COV aircraft were redelivered to RAF units in 2000. Saudi Arabia received twenty-four new ADVs to F3 standard, while Italy leased twenty-four upgraded, ex-RAF F3s from 1995 to the end of 2004, as interim fighters pending arrival of its Typhoons.

In early 1992 it was decided that an interim capability be developed in which production TIALD pods were integrated onto the existing Tornado Advanced Programme (TAP) 2 software. The programme was called interim TIALD capability (ITC), and work started at Boscombe Down in July that year. Over an intense four-week period, including long sorties and lengthy debriefs, new software for both pod and the aircraft were developed, the net result being a capability far in excess of that originally required by SR(A) 1015. The decision was taken to deploy TIALD pods to the Gulf on Operation Jural, this time not to designate bombs, but to provide surveillance of Iraqi military positions south of the 32nd Parallel as the RAF's contribution to Operation Southern Watch, which provided protection for Iraqi Shiites from Saddam Hussein's oppression south of the 32nd Parallel. On 27 August 1992, three crews from 617 Squadron and one crew from 13 Squadron joined crews from II (AC) Squadron in the surveillance role with Tornado GR1/GR1As. Sorties took place by day and night, lasting up to four hours, and apart from the surveillance of ground targets/areas, these included air-to-air refuelling with VC 10s. During training sorties over Kuwait in September 1992, LGBs were released at targets on the Udairi Range with a 100% success rate, proving the capability of the new pods. Operationally, TIALD was again put to the test in January 1993, when Saddam Hussein ventured to put surface-to-air missiles south of the 32nd Parallel. Two missions were carried out, one at night, the other during the day. Three of the four targets assigned were destroyed.

With the disbandment in October 1993 and April 1994 of the two Buccaneer squadrons at Lossiemouth, 12 (as 27 Squadron had been renumbered in October 1993) and 617 Tornado Squadrons took over the maritime/overland strike/attack role by April 1994. As part of the RAF's draw-down of strength in Germany, the reconnaissance GR1As of II (AC) Squadron moved to Marham from Laarbruch, to be followed by the second GR1A unit, 13 Squadron, which arrived from Honington. With the final closure of RAF bases in Germany on 17 July 2001, IX (B) Squadron and 31 Squadron moved with their Tornado GR4s from Brüggen to Marham.

Early in 2001 the *Luftwaffe* had around 270 IDS aircraft in service, including a number to electronic combat and reconnaissance (ECR) standard and armed with AGM-88 HARMs. The aircraft underwent a comprehensive MLU similar to the RAF's GR4 programme that also added Litening targeting pods and towed radar decoys. New weapons included BLU-109 and GBU-22 Paveway III LGBs, KEPD

GR4Bs of 617 'Dam Busters' Squadron and 12 (B) Squadron from RAF Lossiemouth with a Nimrod MR2 over the sea. (MoD)

GR4s of II (AC) Squadron (top left), IX (B) Squadron (top right), 13 Squadron (bottom left) and 31 Squadron (right) of 138 Wing at RAF Marham. (RAF Marham)

350 Taurus tactical cruise missiles and IRIS-T self-defence AAMs. The *Marineflieger* has a wing with around fifty IDS aircraft assigned to conventional attack, anti-shipping (with Kormoran anti-shipping missiles), defence suppression (with HARMs) and reconnaissance missions. The Italian Air Force has three fighter-bomber IDS groups, one of which is assigned the anti-ship role with Kormoran missiles. Italy converted fifteen aircraft to IT ECR standard with dedicated electronic equipment and HARMs for the

defence suppression role. Saudi Arabia is the remaining Tornado operator, with the survivors of ninety-six aircraft assigned to three units, one of which operates twelve reconnaissance-configured Tornadoes.

The RAF's reconnaissance-configured GR1As have been upgraded to GR4As, which are equipped with the reconnaissance airborne pod Tornado (RAPTOR) pod, one of the most advanced reconnaissance sensors in the world, which has greatly increased the effectiveness of the Tornado in the reconnaissance role. RAPTOR has the ability to download real-time, long-range, oblique-photography data to ground stations or to the cockpit during a mission. The stand-off range of the sensors also allows the aircraft to remain outside heavily defended areas, thus minimising the aircraft's exposure to enemy air-defence systems. Even when working tens of miles away from a subject being photographed, RAPTOR is capable of capturing startlingly high-resolution images, even at night. Some Tornado GR4s involved in Operation Telic in Iraq in 2003 were fitted with the RAPTOR pod, and subsequently they were employed in the Gulf on both close-support and reconnaissance missions in support of Coalition forces in Iraq.

RAF IDS Tornadoes operate primarily in the long-range interdiction/overland attack role. They also have specialised missions that comprise maritime attack (GR1B) and reconnaissance (GR1A). In 2001 the RAF began using fully operational GR1s upgraded to GR4 standard with new cockpit displays, full compatibility with the TIALD pod for autonomous precision-guided munitions (PGM) delivery, integration of NVGs with an upgraded forward-looking infra-red (FLIR) and an enhanced self-defence suite. Defensively, the GR4 is normally armed with two

AIM-9L Sidewinder short-range AAMs, a BOZ-107 pod on the right wing to dispense chaff and flares and a Sky Shadow-2 ECM pod on the left wing. The aircraft can also carry an integral 27 mm Mauser cannon capable of firing 1,700 rounds per minute. From 2003 the GR4 has also been equipped with the CASOM/Storm Shadow long-range, stand-off, air-to-ground missile which allows the Tornado to make precision strikes in poor weather with a greatly increased stand-off range from the target area. The Storm Shadow saw operational service in 2003 with 617 Squadron prior to entering full service in 2004. The Brimstone advanced radar-guided missile, which is derived from the US Army Hellfire AGM-114F weapon, went into service on the Tornado GR4 in 2005. It provides the Tornado with an effective anti-armour weapon in all weathers, day and night, and it also provides an enhanced stand-off range. In RAF service a pylon-mounted launching rack contains three Brimstone missiles.

CURRENT RAF TORNADO UNITS

1 Group Air Combat

OCU 15 (R) Squadron	RAF Lossiemouth	12 GR4
12 (B) Squadron	RAF Lossiemouth	12 GR4B
14 Squadron	RAF Lossiemouth	12 GR4
617 'Dam Busters' Squadron	RAF Lossiemouth	12 GR4B
II (AC) Squadron	RAF Marham	12 GR4A
IX (B) Squadron	RAF Marham	12 GR4
13 Squadron	RAF Marham	12 GR4A
31 Squadron	RAF Marham	12 GR4
25 (F) Squadron	RAF Leeming	16 F3
43 (F) Squadron	RAF Leuchars	16 F3
56 (Reserve) Squadron	RAF Leuchars	16 F3
111 (F) Squadron	RAF Leuchars	16 F3
1435 Flight	Falklands Isles	4 F3
Fast-jet & Guided Weapons OEU	RAF Coningsby	3 F3/2 GR4

Profiles of Flight

PANAVIA TORNADO

GR1, GR1P, GR4, GR4A, IDS, ECR, F3

Tornado F3 MM7234 '36-24' of *36°Stormo 12°Gruppo*
Aeronautica Militare Italiano
(Ex ZE167. Transferred to the *AMI* in 1997)

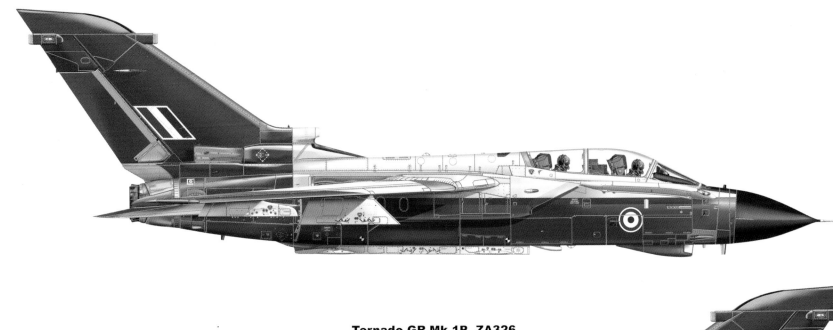

Tornado GR.Mk 1P ZA326
of the **Defence Evaluation & Research Agency**
2005

Tornado GR.Mk 4A ZA401 'XIII' of No.13 Squadron
90th anniversary 1915 – 2005

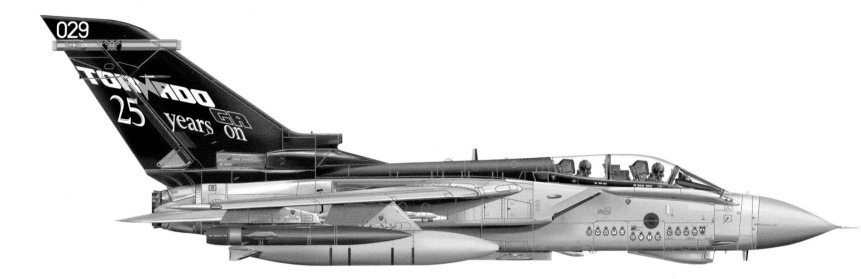

Tornado GR.Mk 4 ZA469 '029' of No.9 Squadron
Tornado GR 25th anniversary 2007

Tornado GR.Mk 4 ZA543 'FF' of No.12 Squadron
90th anniversary 1915 – 2005

Tornado GR.Mk 1 ZA560
of the **Tri-national Tornado Training Establishment**
Display aircraft 1995

Tornado GR.Mk 4 ZA564 of **No.31 Squadron**
90th anniversary 1915 – 2005

Tornado GR.Mk 4 ZD748 of **No.2 Squadron**
95th anniversary 1912 – 2007

Tornado GR.Mk 4 ZG756 'BX' of **No.14 Squadron**
90th anniversary 1915 – 2005

Tornado IDS MM7005 of *36°Stormo 156°Gruppo*
Aeronautica Militare Italiano
Tornado IDS 60,000 flight hours 2007

Tornado IDS MM7006 '6-31' of *6°Stormo 154°Gruppo*
Aeronautica Militare Italiano
Tornado IDS 25th anniversary 2007

Tornado IDS 43+96 of *Aufklarungsgeschwader 51 'Immelmann'*
Luftwaffe
Nato Tiger Meet 2004

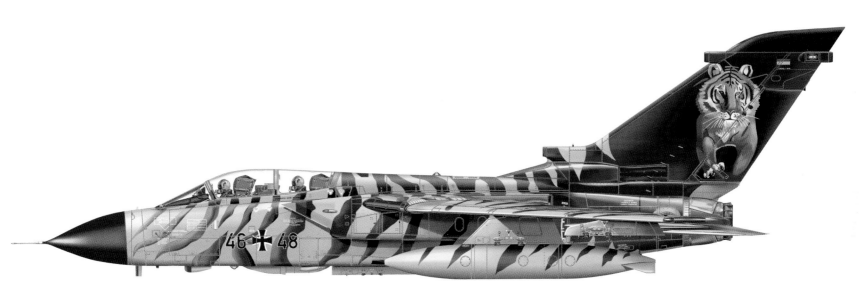

Tornado ECR 46+48 of *321 Staffel, Jagdbombergeschwader 32*
Luftwaffe
Nato Tiger Meet 2007

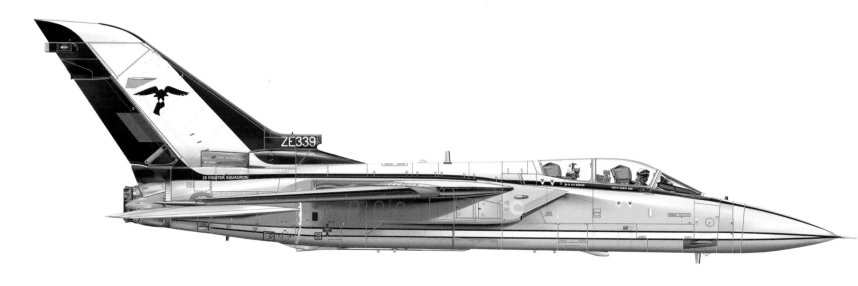

Tornado F.Mk 3 ZE339 of **No.25 Squadron**
Strike Command Tornado display aircraft 1991

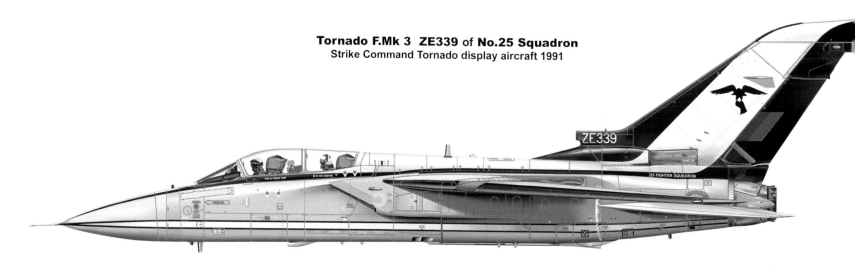

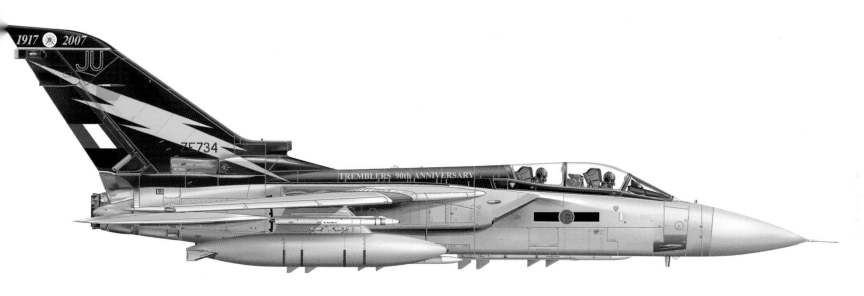

Tornado F.Mk 3 ZE734 'JU' of No.111 Squadron
90th anniversary 1917 – 2007

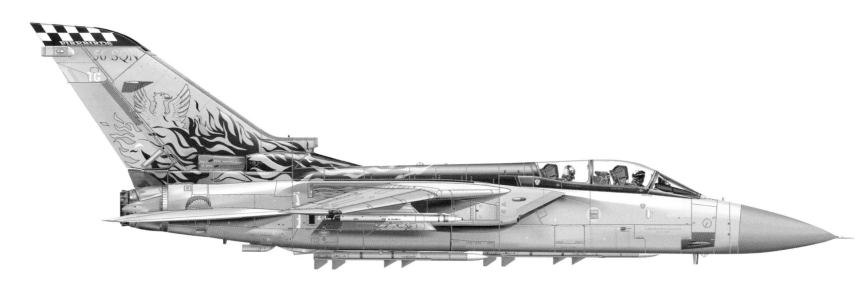

Tornado F.Mk 3 ZE735 'TG' of No.56 (Reserve) Squadron
90th anniversary 1917 – 2007

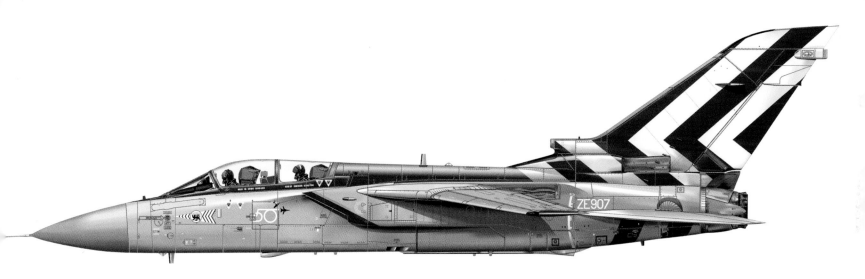

Tornado F.Mk 3 ZE907 of **No.65 (Reserve) Squadron**
No.229 Operational Conversion Unit
50th anniversary of the Battle of Britain 1990

Tornado F.Mk 3 ZG757 of No.43 Squadron
90th anniversary 1916 – 2006